More
POEMS
for
HUNGRY
MINDS

2024

Other books by

HIGHLAND AVENUE POETS

The Social Distance
2020

Poems for Hungry Minds
2022

More
POEMS
for
HUNGRY
MINDS

2024

A Publication of HIGHLAND AVENUE POETS

Birmingham, Alabama

Steve Coleman, Managing Editor

Address all inquiries to:
highlandavepoets@gmail.com.

Illustrations by Véronique Vanblaere
Cover photo by Tom Gordon

Cover and interior design by The Book Cover Whisperer:
OpenBookDesign.biz

979-8-9869814-4-4 Paperback
979-8-9869814-3-7 Hardcover
979-8-9869814-5-1 eBook

FIRST EDITION

Available at Amazon and IngramSpark

Contents

PREFACE

WHY POETRY?

As many people write poetry as read it. A successful "poetry reading" is one where there are more people in the audience than on the stage.

The easiest way to clear a room is to announce, "Now I would like to read you a poem I wrote."

Poetry is a gift that comes with the burden of reading, thinking, and, God forbid, feeling.

Don't even think about remuneration. Unlike teaching or other charitable pursuits, it is not even a graceful way to starve.

A little over 10 years ago, I invited a couple of friends over to drink wine (theirs) and eat bad cooking (mine) with the excuse of reading poetry (theirs, mine and anyone else's we cared to present) and talking about "anything other than Alabama football. "

Everyone was invited to bring a friend who seemed compatible with the group, and the dinners took place more or less once a month, with the understanding that they would continue until the earlier of loss of interest or death by food poisoning.

I confess that I had two entirely selfish motives: First, I was tired of poetry groups that met to trade platitudes among people more interested in being told how well they wrote than how they could write better. Given the lack of other rewards, ego massage is often the only excuse for chasing the Muse.

The second was a vague notion of hosting a salon: one of those turn-of-the-century gatherings where one might find, for example, Freud, Klimt, Schiele, Mahler, Rokitansky (a progenitor of science-based medicine) and sharing interdisciplinary insights and, I suppose, looking for some justification for their commitment to their respective fields.*

As I hoped, we had great fun, and the group winnowed itself down over the years to those who earnestly wanted to improve in what can only be described as a hobby, somewhat more exciting than stamp collecting and less strenuous than rock climbing: Learning to express oneself and communicate to others the true nature of experience, emotion, insight, and, often, utter confusion at the world around us.

We lost three wonderful friends and talented writers to one of the most confusing of these topics, mortality. Brian, Charlie and Chervis— Charlie and Chervis being represented in these pages and Brian having been featured in our earlier anthology, *Poems for Hungry Minds*.

Others drifted away, either due to a lack of commitment or interest, or, perhaps, despair at the cuisine and conversation.

Due to Covid (topic of our first anthology, The Social Distance), the group moved to monthly and later semi-monthly online meetings and the focus shifted to poetry *uber alles*.

What follows is a selection of work we produced or refined in recent months, exhibiting, I think, the benefit of our interaction. It is with great pride and no small amount of ego satisfaction that I say the Highland Avenue Poets have gone far beyond anything I could have hoped, both in terms of ability and commitment to one of the hardest and most precious of human endeavors: creating art with little hope of fame, fortune, or any benefit other than looking at the page and murmuring, "Yep, that is what I wanted to say."

Thank you, readers, for opening these pages. I sincerely hope you will find your time well spent. Thank you, poets, for the years of your time, insight, friendship, patience ... and strong stomachs.

Barry Marks

P.S. Each of the poets who contributed to this book wants to thank Steve Coleman for his hard work and wise counsel in the planning, editing, assembling, overseeing printing, author-herding, and ego-taming that made this anthology possible.

*see Kandel, The Age of Insight.

Ars Poetica

So This Metaphor

So This Metaphor
jumps the track and escapes
the narrative of his poem;
son of a gun
dances between the shadows
like something of moonlight
and lands on top of a girl
pretty as a promise.

When he makes a stupid joke
about enjambment,
she laughs and tells him
he's more entertaining
than that poet she's dating.

"No," the poet sighs. *"You've missed*
The point by a metric foot.
Now get back on the page."

But the emancipated metaphor
just mutters something about
not being born for a villanelle
and *"all net, no tennis."*
He slips off to live
in the imaginary forest
of forgotten imagery.

~ Barry Marks

Stream of Humanity

It's time to say our few words because
tomorrow our soul sets sail.
— George Seferis,
"An Old Man on the River Bank"

My Greek friend's poems flow from him
Like a rain-swollen river, unchecked,
Irresistible, quenching a
Thirst he first felt late in life.
His poems contain arresting tropes,
English verse enlivened by
Greek-born imagery, as wild herbs
Elevate taverna sardines.

He self-deprecates (a peasant ploy):
"But I am uneducated." Yet why wouldn't
Homer's muse strike someone blessed
With his earthy energy, granting him
The lyrical license known to
The ancient epic-spinners, to
Shepherds singing to their flocks.

On the terrace of his whitewashed
House in the Peloponnese hills,
I sip muddy coffee as morning mist
Retreats, unveiling gnarled olive trees.
I'm reading a poem by the celebrated
Seferis, the old man of the title.
It draws wisdom from the Nile,
The river that is all rivers. He
Gazed across its watery chasm
In Cairo; like our electric laureate,
He sat on that bank of sand
And watched the river flow.

My prolific friend shares
His second poem of the day.
Aimed, it seems, at seduction
(poetry's first purpose?), it evokes
The spark of desire that Zeus hurled
From Olympus, wreaking havoc
Among gods and mortals.
But of course: With twinkling eyes,
His curly hair ash-gray but his libido
Ember-bright, still catnip to the ladies,
He recalls lusty statues of Pan
In the National Museum.
Surely his shoes conceal

Cloven hooves.

Poetry can also bear the weight of history:
Seferis refused to publish
While the junta ruled, until finally,
Wreathed in cigarette smoke and the
Nobel laurel, he broke his silence
To denounce the colonels,
Their abyss of oppression.
It emboldened the nation.
When he died a few months later,
Thousands marched with his coffin
To the grave, a mass demonstration
Sanctioned by grief, for a man
Of honor and his country.

~ JEFF BOOK

I HOTE POETRY

The first line fumbled off fat fingers,
But the Freudian flip slips and lingers.
To let fate direct a better, more cozy melody.
Placing "hote" where "hate" might be.

"Hote" is such a harsh word, (something now
editorially endowed),
To quench a word-ly hungering, with that which is
righter vowelled.
Methinks it dines on familiar whines, when mind and red
wine fails
A prayer for lither emotive expresses for new, dye-blackened trails.

In the mouth, I might punch thee, bard, for being oh
so-Shakespeare
Thy inkish stream babbles dewy softness, from which mine
often veer.
On the page, thou dance with words, that seemingly struggle not.
In lands I thought I fought, for words elusive, effusive, lost
and sought.

And I strain, intransigent, on weak letters and signs, the
movements minor, in iotas.
And return to begin and begin to return, entreated by these sexy,
literary codas.
From hote to home, I've blustered on porch, shouting to related,
passersby poetic.
I pray genuflection, dull pen to unforgiving paper, generates
inspiration kinetic.

It matters all, I suspect, the summit, depth, literary flowerings and expressive blight …
Be present in this hote word then, Amen, and in the next ones, nay better ones, I may write.

~ MEL CAMPBELL

SCRAPS

The Serengeti preserve has been
more or less returned to nature,
per Tennyson, *red in tooth and claw.*

Scavengers needed. Apply here.
No experience necessary.
Someone has to clean up this mess.

Buzzards and birds are clear volunteers.
From lofty branches they peer
down, waiting for someone to die.

But the real work of death takes place on
 the ground, where Hyena and Jackal wait
for the big cats to finish.

The Hyena stinks of death from 50 feet,
and relies on carrion but will eat
the wounded that still breathe.

The dapper Jackal, clever canine, waits
for Lions to finish. There will come another day.
Yet the Hyena won't go hungry; the Jackal may.

We poets are scavengers ourselves –
stealing off with metaphor sopping from our muzzles,
also as per Tennyson, *a world of plunder and prey.*

We who read everything are sponges with short recall
of whence that phrase or idea came; invention from
a month past still colors our shirts with stain.

Dismissed by many as having a dull hobby,
Well, it's not like writing a novel.
No, it is not.

How many lines can you cite from a book?
Now a poem.
To be a scavenger is noble.

What once *was* may never be entirely lost,
but kept in trust by those
who dare to set a page on fire.

~ J. SHANNON WEBSTER

IMMORTALITY

– to John Keats

To write one poem
Remembered
Long after I am gone—
     Though I will not
     Be present to listen
     As students recite it—
That would be enough.

~ JIM FERGUSON

Nature

NELLITA DAWN

Cool morning mist recumbent on Hood Canal
Surface tickled by sprinkles and ripples of minnows.
Smooth pebbled shores overrun by tides,
Leaves and limbs of alders drip dewy green.
Old eagle's claws grip wet branch,
His feathers now specked with yellowed gray,
On vigil countless days,
Waiting and wondering if breakfast appears.
A small, unwary salmon rises
In laze unaware on sea salty surface.
Worn wings, groaning, unfold and flap,
Slow-motion swoop, watery crash,
Fish escapes, skitters away.
Creaking back to his perch,
Limbs swaying, he lands,
Stands proud awaiting, glaring,
"You too, old man, do understand."
Him there, me here, we watch sun rise,
Glistening distant snowy Olympic peaks
Emerging from mist and ever-gentle rain.

~ STEVE COLEMAN

BIRDS FLY TOGETHER

Ever flickering V-shaped silhouettes
at 40, 50 miles an hour, tumbling paired loops,
kinetic joy, swarms of birds, pouring sheafs of identical
black grains against bright clouds.

There is no way to tell one bird from another,
nor to watch them do anything other than
zoom from place to place, although sometimes,
if the swifts are flying low over ancient
clay London rooftops,

I see one open its huge gaping mouth,
turning the bird into something
like an alligator. Watching them with
the naked eye is rewarding,
it reveals explosiveness in what was blankness.

Swifts pay attention to what other
swifts are doing,
follow one another, band together,
connect like no other species.

Swifts fly higher
to sleep on the wind,
they can put half of their brain to sleep,
with the other half awake while they fly.

Next day, they're back, one hundred swifts
circling high, purposefully as bees in a hive,
never landing, never stoping,
never losing their life force, always free.

Already the frozen door of the North closes,
strength and purpose rises in the collaboration
of these numberless strong
and multitudinous souls.

~ ROGER CARLISLE

HERON

[For my friend, Gates Shaw]

Sun falling, shadows bold.
Water reflecting last light,
motored down river.
Friend sat still,
staring
at light slivers
on trees, shadows
fading
into
darkness.

I turned where
heron sat. Still,
staring, taking in
approaching night.

No words spoken.
Yet we were told.

~ NICK GAEDE

WOODLANDS

crown shyness forms
rivers and borders
aloft in the canopy

reticent trees
sway in the dance
close but not touching

like lovers-to-be
moving in concert
rooted yet seeking

union of limbs
trunks and torsos
dropping all leaves

touching the sky

~ JIM FERGUSON

GREENING OF THE TREES

More than the showy flowers,
the obscene display of cherry blossom pink,

it's the greening of the trees that really
ignites a fire in my belly.

No joy in the purple python wisteria
choking, creeping loudly.

No celebration in the the ecstasy of falling sensual
catkins across the landscape.

An intense yellow fire explodes inside the forest green
of each leaf.

When the momentary shock of white, red and pink flowers
passes on, I feel the persistent throb of green leaves

calling me to listen and watch in awe.
It's the green, the green, the verdant green.

~ ROGER CARLISLE

Patagonia by Air

Something fishy there is about a
flood of North American anglers
pouring into Patagonia pursuing trout.

We fly south to Balmaceda on an
A321, aiming for the end of the world:
Simpson River and a fly-fisher's dream.

My compatriots are executive fry,
buoyant and dripping with net worth,
as they perch on the arms of their seats.

I shun affinity, flounder to look Chilean.
The lads are hooked on a company trip
I've envied for fifty years.

Through the window the Andes' vertical
escarpments clutch at the ether. Light
varies blue to red, reliant on wavelength.

The barrens below break rugged and sere,
and scattered electric blue lakes appear to be
stamped out by a divine mad cookie cutter.

I did not know, on the plane, that in two days
I would be (save the guide) blessedly alone,
holding a Rainbow long as my arm.

~ J. SHANNON WEBSTER

Rainbows Unseen
Still Fly Colors

In this Deep South city
Spring comes on like
An ardent hooligan, horny
And spoiling for a fight,
Its weather biblical, bipolar.
The sun arcs higher, longer,
Lighting the green fuse
Waiting patiently in plants.
Monsoons choke sump pumps
And low crossings, sweeping away
Cars and shallow-minded drivers.
Gentle days coax forsythia and
Lenten roses to brave late freezes.
Birds rut in song, trilling and thrilling
Like jazzmen in a cutting contest.
Gusty nights stiffen daffodil spines
And test trees' greening lacework.

On every month's first Wednesday
The tornado sirens sing, keening
Their doomsday din in the gravid air.
Brother, they toll for thee—take heed,
And when it's not a test, take cover.
Or else, like me, fill your lungs with
Charged oxygen and witness the storm
From the opera box of your porch,
Absorbing the erotics of atmosphere
As drops fly, wires thrum, and
Tall trees hum and sway
Side to side like a gospel choir.

In this riotous arena, the sky glowers
Darkly, a vessel for the crackling lightning
And booming thunder of parading storms,
Ingenues that race the weatherman's pulse,
Drop his barometric pressure, and
Excite him to doff his coat and draw
Anxious lines on the radar map,
Shadowboxing with Mother Nature.

Storm-front winds snatch our recycling,
Cartwheeling cans and pirouetting paper.
Plastic bags jitterbug in the air.
A possum gives birth in a dumpster,
Both shelter and buffet; somehow she
Knows to escape with her brood before
The trash truck upends her nest.

Pollen wreaths festoon our drunken-sailor
Sidewalks—cracked, root-heaved,
Demanding attention, as if designed
By an agility trainer, or a therapist sure
That balance tests forestall dementia.
Crazy-quilt concrete, a metaphor underfoot:
Life's path is uneven, be nimble, try to keep up.

Spring sunshine is a lover's caress
That ends too soon, as the rain,
Pleasant or pelting, carries on,
Showers flowers, sluices gutters,
Sows rainbows and revival,
Refreshing the weary world.

~ JEFF BOOK

CHILDREN

Four Bluebird babies just left home.

I watched them grow, watched their parents
feed them, remove their poop in white sacs.

From the moment they hatched
until the moment they fledged,
they were safe.

Their home was security
in pine needles, grass strands, and wood.
Untouched by lightning,
unruffled by thunder,
unflinching atop a pole,
protected by a baffle
and a rain-resistant roof,
with parental beaks a constant
conveyor of larvae, insect thoraxes, heads and abdomens.

Security became less certain
when the babies made their fluffy, unsteady exits.
Windows, cats, hawks, pavement on habitat
are just some of the threats they will face
on their flight path to adulthood and nest-building.

With luck, they will live for six to 10 years.

With luck, they and their offspring
will never feel the blow of a bomb
or the scream from the sky that heralds its arrival.

Children in Ukraine and Gaza have no such guarantee.

~ TOM GORDON

SPRING

Just as we give in
to cold days, grey clouds of winter,
she walks in, a surprise visitor.

A hippie in a tie dyed dress,
dancing to a Lady Ga Ga song,
carrying baskets of sunshine,
soft April rains, honey suckle wreaths;
wildflowers in her hair.

She sends white pollen to watch over us,
as the earth dresses itself in green,
the sun decides to warm our hearts,
gardens surprise us with color.

We throw off our coats,
put on shorts and bare feet,
open our arms,
and ask her to dance.

~ ROGER CARLISLE

WONDER

Bud on limb.
Shoots upward.
Folds open.
Seeks sun.
Observes moon.
Watches bees,
crickets, squirrels
spring by in delight.

Shadows extend.
Becomes dry, bright,
folds inward. Wind
twists grip. Floats
in a dream. Rides
updraft to escape.
Rests on cool ground.

~ NICK GAEDE

LEECHES

For Ben, during his treatment for a toe infection

And in those days, for this affliction,
One might be prescribed
A simple course of leeches
To remove the evils that
slither through your veins
and afflict your unseen wound.

The leeches swim ready, hoping for
the now-forgotten physics' call,
to mend limb and mind, as they did
before amoxicillin or alcohol
Or hot pokers...
To cleanly, neatly suck death from life.

Instead, you sit, in chair
Reclined and reverse bled,
Infused with modern bacterial assassins for
the tiniest of demons dancing neath your skin.

Forty-three treatments, Christ's temptation
And three more days,
With the son, the father (watching)
And a temporary, holey spigot
in your arm
to baptize your bones
with high-tech holy water
and exercise "Legion" from your toe.

Trusting in modern medicine -- clean, sterile,
where polite, informed conversations,
are held in boring, vanilla-flavored offices;
where loaf bread definitions of devilments
are delivered by doctors in dockers...
And blood is scientifically spilled,
shots fired into skin and
pain inflicted and subdued.

And we writhe --
at the thought of ancient
barbers bleeding our brothers
to improve the complexion
or strain out the eviler humors
of our nature;
at ignorance plied in
honest earnestness
that, in faith, poked a hopeful thumb
in the weathering dam of demise.

There, but for grace, to receive the best
that ancient medicine had to offer.
And nevertheless, thankful, for the best
of our current age …
Yet, I wonder, as the drip slips
into my son's arm, if future patients
will thank the maker
that they do not have to endure
the unfathomable
treatments of our today.

~ MEL CAMPBELL   31

ODE TO THE OYSTER

Consider the oyster,
That briny éclair:
Armored nugget,
Nacreous engine,
Prodigious filter,
Muscle of shoals.
Figment of tide and time.

Imagine evolution had
Spawned mega oysters.
They'd have cobbled inlets.
Hobbled harbors, and
Needed a crowbar
And saw to shuck—a
Walrus and a carpenter.
Yielding colossal pearls,
Gazing balls for a
Sultan's garden.

But the brave man
Who first ate an oyster
Found a morsel fit
To savor and slurp—
Like sex, a moist act
Of mutual surrender.
Fuel for love, or so
Believe many
Fools for love.

Near the shore
By homes of yore,
Shells heaped high showed
Affluence and ease,
The bounty of a salty Eden.
Now they're seeding
A billion oysters around
New York, once and future
Metropolis of mollusks,
With oyster bars
Above and below
The tidal flow.

Shucked but not shocked
(Yet seeming to quiver):
The bride laid bare,
A gleam in a hungry eye.
Bivalve primeval,
Never truculent,
Always succulent,
The oyster abides.
Its flesh sustains
And sings of the sea.

~ JEFF BOOK

CLOUDS

In Alaska one day
venture out at Skagway.
Up mountain, clouds
large and small play.

Glacier white/grey-
Blue, far away. River
below, snow patches
above glitter in sun.

As day comes to an end
small clouds nestle
to hills, while
mountain peaks play hide
and seek with larger clouds
who like night cover
all as in a shroud.

~ NICK GAEDE

NOT POETIC

When coral sea fans bleach,
While western rains waste,
And lakes become Aral,
How can anyone claim to be poetic?

Humans abuse our only planet;
Agribusinesses turn a big profit:
While on parched, sere land
Dirt farmers starve.

I try now to turn a poesy bit
As the wild beasts and the fish
Diminish and decline by degree--
Starving and sick from too much heat.

The subjects of poetry,
Professor Mason once said,
Are only love and death;
And love barely qualifies.

Write on about love then
And in bliss bathe yourself.
Live in the moment of love
And fail to see what's coming.

For this planet and those
Who believe love is eternal,
Not only your heart warms--
But the biome bakes.

~ STEVE COLEMAN

Society

The Daily Unanswered

Good morning.
Hey, how are you?
What's going on?
Excuse me, I'm walking behind you.
That's a lovely blouse.
Cool color on those sandals.
How old is your baby?
Don't I know you?
Would you like one of these?
What kind of dog is that?
May I pet it?

Good afternoon.
I think you dropped something.
Beautiful singing voice,
may I join you?
May I help you carry that?
I'm passing you on the left!
Please don't throw that on the ground.
I've got an extra napkin if you need it.
What book are you reading?
Hey, I'm a Cardinal fan, too.
Fine-looking dog. What's its name?

Good evening.

Hey, it's me, it's me, your friend Tom!

Did you see that heron spear that crawfish?

Do you know everyone in the gym just heard you break wind?

Ahh, look at that pup.

Hello? You're walking into my cycling path!

Hello?

Hello?

I was saying ….. Nice earbuds.

~ TOM GORDON

HIJACKER

A robo-call came today:
"True Christians must vote!"
Claiming theirs the only hope against
evil fomented by the Other Side.
"We are right. They are wrong,"
the robotic caller said,
"Respond to your Christian duty!"

Ending the call, I sought to unpack,
asking what's Christian
about implying that
liberal tolerance is evil?
What are the tenets
of his self-serving belief?
Faith, hope, charity surely
find no dominion there.

It's not new, this sort of hate.
Religion distorted, perverted,
supplanted by baseless conspiracy theories:
ANTIFA, QANON,
condemning as sin
brown or black skin.

Your moral compass has precessed--
fallen quite out of its gimbals.
I see through you.
I denounce you and
your twisted ethic.

You will not
hijack my Jesus
 to further your own
selfish, self-righteous
political aims.

~ STEVE COLEMAN

ROWING REVERIE

My mate Tim is crossing the Channel,
Stroke by stroke, on a rowing machine.
Not on some screen but in his head:
The white cliffs recede, low fog burns off,
Mewling gulls hover and dart.
Embarked on an incremental journey,
He is one of an armada of strivers
Launched by a fitness challenge.
Grip tethered to a flywheel, he yoyos
Back and forth on the sliding seat,
Bound for the beaches of Normandy
From the warmth of a Devonshire gym.

On this side of the pond, I row too,
On the very same machine,
Not sure what I'm crossing—the
Delaware, perhaps, cleaving river ice
To help Washington rout the Hessians.
The Styx, churning away from Hell.
The Bosporus, lapping East and West.
Or a mountain lake, so mirror-still that
My oar blades shard the sky and
Drive bubbles down, out of sight.

It's a moving meditation.
The body finds a steady rhythm
All parts working together,
Function shaping form,
To and fro, the resisting fan
Whipping up an offshore breeze.

This rowing on dry land
Echoes something ancient.
Sea-scything oars powered
Viking longboats, slave galleys, the
Greek triremes that wreaked havoc
On the Persian fleet at Salamis.

Like Earth's surface, we are
Ourselves mostly water, long after
We came ashore and traded
Flippers for limbs.
We are destined to row,
Like whalers in hot pursuit,
Aiming to harpoon fortune.

For a crew in perfect unison,
Rowing is more poetry than sport.
Earbuds in place—Sirens shall not
lure me to my doom!—I absorb
Cautionary tales, buoyant interviews,
Cultural flotsam, desert island discs.
(Marooned, could I row to my rescue?)
At least I cannot capsize.

Other rowers mount nearby machines
Merge with and animate them,
Moving back and forth, shuttlecocks
Weaving fitness on castaway looms.
Agents of repetition (the gist of all gyms).
Harness our energy, capture our joules,
And what progress we could power.
With the lazy 8 in my sights,
I will row to infinity.

~ JEFF BOOK

EXPIRATION DATE

I am not the mother of a new-born,
a sentinel at the ready with comforting words and caresses
when cries come from the nursery.

I am not a prison chaplain,
a prayerful presence in the life of one condemned
as his end draws near.

Tonight, I am an eager executioner,
my ears on hair trigger alert for the thrashing racket
you will make when you are lodged in the sticky trap
where lies the rest of the apple cake
you shredded from its aluminum wrapper last night.

Now that I hear you, I rise,
with no soothing sounds to put you at ease,
only the weaponized whisper,
I am going to rid the world of you.
You signed the warrant last night
with a trail of crumb-covered glitter on the porch.

I was careless to leave the cake exposed.
Now you are exposed.
While I am puzzled as to how you got in,
I know with certainty how you are going out.
I am the governor of this house,
and I am not in the business of last-minute reprieves.

~ TOM GORDON

Justice Puzzle

(For Doug Jones)

Why did we wait

to try the man

so filled with hate,

who spoke and acted

violence?

Garbled

senseless words.

Spewed years before

that grate

more now

than then.

When pieces there
we could not
would not
piece together.
Pieces lost
or missing, but he
pondered, prayed,
moved pieces there
to here.

"Let me show
how puzzle
now complete".
Stage set yet
some opine"If not guilty then
how guilty now."

I thought but
hesitated to say,
"If guilty then,
guilty now."

Why did we wait?

~ NICK GAEDE

POPS

The ducks were gone
from the park pond,
but the geese were back.
A man fished from the bank,
folks dined outdoors
across the street,
and a few strollers
circled the pond
on a paved path
in the plodding pace
of a lazy Sunday.

I watched it all
from a hillside perch,
calmed by the pond's
ripple-free reflection
of the sky overhead,
hearing little
but the light whoosh of traffic,
an occasional goose squawk,
and words wafting up
from the paved path.

I did not expect
the abrupt arrival
of distant pops,
but they came on fast,
like someone stomping
a balloon bouquet.

Then they were gone,
leaving a residual echo
of anxious anticipation.

A minute later,
their tripwire breached,
sirens began
their insistent, frantic blare.

~ TOM GORDON

DUAL PANDEMICS

Slithering on surfaces touched,
Riding unmasked air deep into lungs
Spiked viral globes launch an attack.
Covid kills without caring
Whether skin is white, brown, or black.

Yet while Corona virus sickens--
A heartless scourge murdering,
Hundreds of thousands in our nation,
A second quite deadly disease
Causes all great consternation.

Those Americans of white European linage
Unconsciously fear competing with other races.
Afraid of losing their place in society,
They suppress all non-whites in racial disparity,
Keeping them down in near poverty.

Emotions transform fear into hate,
Facts grow, distorted by rationalization;
Fear-mongered and confused about how to feel,
Maskless violators of sequestered protection believe it's just political,
While malevolent trolls claim Antifa and Qanon are real.

Befuddled, enraged and insurrection-crazed,
Demagogue-driven, endemically infected,
Seeking ethnic dominance in a Caucasian Eden--
Misguided, bewildered, worshipping a false god--
They dream of a past which never has been.

Thankfully, medical scientists have discovered vaccines

To inoculate from Covid-19.

But misguided hate, untruth rage uncured.

Can national leaders create a lifesaving serum

To cure the manipulated, confused, hate-sickened deluded?

~ STEVE COLEMAN

PEACEFUL SPOT

These jewels among
Flanders Fields of
turnips and sugar beets.
Off autoroute to back
roads one must go to
look upon row after row
white stone crosses
upright white markers
interrupting green lawn
edges sharp and clean.
Flowers intertwine with stones
over resting shattered bones.

Are blades greener, more erect?
Are flowers less muted, more pure?

Because Holy One shines upon
      Seven
            Thousand
                  Three Hundred
     And One Two Three Four
And upon you and me who
      Look
            Are thankful
                 Then move on.

~ NICK GAEDE

No Mark, No Crater

(Fall, 2022)

An acorn falls from an oak,
hits my exposed wrist
and tumbles to the street,
where it bounces and rolls.

My wrist hurts. But only a little.
As though a crawfish pincer
had found my skin.

I still have the wrist.
Can still flex it.
The nut has left
no lasting mark, no crater
in my path.
No need for sirens, stretchers,
or hasty hands with bandages.

If only it were acorns falling in Ukraine.

~ Tom Gordon

LEADING LIGHTS

Life is like sailing,
Sailing's like life--
Pleasures and challenges,
Each offers its strife.
Coming home at night
Amid fierce wind and wave,
From sea to safe harbor
What man doesn't pray?

As an aid to sailors,
One tall light on the shore
With another much lower,
Both sight-aligned
By weary sailors
Coming home from the sea,

Passing wave-crashed rocky quays,
These Leading lights make a range--
And a guide to safe ways.

Yet, often at night,
In the gloom of life
A background of glare
From too many wrong lights,

Causes chaos, confusion, Hazards abound,
Thunderous breakers
Echo terrible sound.

Too many false beacons
Cast pale over truth;
Veracity obscured by
Dark eddies of lies,
Whirlpools of spin,
Demagoguery and fear
Confusing vulnerable men.

We mariners who navigate
High seas and the shoals,
Passing rocky falsehoods,
Distinguish true Leading
From the Lying Lights.
As we sail on, with the devil to pay,
Who will guide us to harbor,
Via secure fairway?

~ STEVE COLEMAN

Cycles of Life

Harvest Time

Three farmers came in from their fields
to find their fathers' friend at home
and wish him well on this his ninetieth
birthday—and then disappear about
as quickly as they had appeared, one
by one, returning to combines, loaders,
balers, bins, dryers and grain, more grain,
miles of golden grain for reaping—
but friends count for much—
and friendship runs deep like Ohio topsoil.
Take care of friends and kin, take time,
Cultivate, and look, the harvest comes.

~ Jim Ferguson

GOING IN CIRCLES

In my garden I rotate like a clock hand,
My dial a broad stone path, its diameter
Large enough to make one revolution
A contemplative stroll past bee-kissed
Flowers in their late-summer heyday.
Like spectators at Ascot, their finery
Upstages the action on the track.
I walk the path with the deliberate calm
Of monks in a cloister, retracing the steps
Of long-gone brothers, treading
Worn stones, meditation in motion.
My dogs follow for a while, then wander
Off-piste, sniffing realms unseen.

In a success-bent society, going in
Circles means going nowhere, as if life
Were an erratic graph, not an endless
Cycle: seed to flowers, cuttings to mulch,
Season to season, the earth round the sun.
No slithering serpent but an ourobouros,
Ancient, tail-devouring, skin-shedding,
Always renewing, world without end.
A circle, like the inner tubes we rode
In spring down the Gunpowder River,
Twirling and shrieking at icy splashes.
Tibetan monks make round mandalas,

Composed with colored sands, their
Intricacies to be erased by the same
Gusts that snap prismatic prayer flags
On the Himalayan plateau. Mt. Kailish,
Four miles high, sacred to four religions,
Glows like an uncut, snow-frosted gem.
Climbing it is taboo—but God is also below.
Pilgrims trek around the base, clockwise
Or counter, according to their faith.
In the thin air existence feels ethereal.

At night the dogs take me for a walk.
In the garden, a soft gray tapestry in the
Moonlight, I improvise a dervish dance,
Giving it a whirl along the round path.
After too much sitting, the body blooms.
Like the flowers, my gaze turns skyward.
I circle the holy mountain, hovering
Above me in the spectral light, a vision
Fed by rising wind, rustling flora, and
My canine avatars, who by nature
Always live in the moment.

~ JEFF BOOK

Dust Motes

Dust motes drifting on sunbeams
once entertained me in my bed.
I would awake to play —
a lion cub learning to wrestle.
I built a blanket fort
for solitude and safe imagination.
At dusk I sought the Evening Star
which waited for my wishes.

On some day I don't remember
my blanket fortress fell.
The universe intruded with lessons
of losses and wounds, and the difference
between truth and myth,
a difference I forget.
But truth comes uninvited
to suggest that at my best,

      my very best,

I may just be a dust mote,
drifting on a sunbeam
for the amusement of a child.

~ Ed Wilson

AT FRIEND'S BEACH HOUSE

Wandered out to beach.
Sandpipers at water's edge
hunting food. Raced up
beach when wave disrupted.
With quick steps returned
as wave receded.

Returned to house, picture
on wall proclaimed--
"Shed your shell."
Words for crabs, shrimp,
other sea creatures.
Our shells harden each
day, rarely shed.

Then these words on wall--
"Leave crabby behind."
Who was crabby first,
me, wife, you, friend?
Ends with regret, silent
or spoken. Time wasted.

Next picture jolts—
"Respect (because
It is fragile)." Yes, it is. Like
sandpipers at water's edge.
As we race about do we
respect others, different
from us? Do we respect
ourselves? Do we
recognize how
fragile all is.

~ NICK GAEDE

TABLE TALK

When we play gin (*yes, I discarded that six*)
I am reminded what a game of gathering it is
(*No, I dealt the last hand, it's your turn now*)
Vertical runs in one suit, or triples of one kind
(*Does a ten count as a face card or a number?*)
And risk-taking, to pick up the growing discards
Or pull from the dwindling stockpile on my turn
(*Rats! I knew you'd be waiting for that ace!*)

The inevitable dispute over rules arises
(*You can't call Rum when you played the card!*)
And simultaneously we think of calling your Mom,
Who knew the rules, and made-up half of them,
(*Remember how she would get so tickled? How
She laughed until she could hardly breathe!*)
Then we listen as you shuffle
The cards falling and filling the silence.

The pace of play slows, speeds up, slows again
Our score so close as we deal the old deck—
The one missing the queen of hearts—
(*We really ought to buy a new pack*)
A joker was doctored long ago to take its place
(*Did one of the kids draw that face?*)
We bask in the memories, and then "ding"—
(*How about a warm brownie? Oh, absolutely!*)

~ JIM FERGUSON

ALUMNUS CUM DOLORE

Visiting the lake beside
Indian Springs School,
forever boy sits
beneath waving willow fronds
overhanging the shore
a sigh shared with the breeze

Watching rippled reflections
O'er-washing deep memories
of growing, learning,
bursting-blood energy of youth

Once seventeen,
now eighty and more
Desperate to return
to what awakened my mind
What I knew
and did not know

To do over not alter--
relieve and relive

Aged in long life
a heart reawakened
aching and breaking
for what once was

~ STEVE COLEMAN

THE

The precedes some word lost before my sentence ends.

The hangs

in space between us as I search my messy box of nouns
to find a name more specific than thingamajig.

The, a single syllable, but definite, demanding
I step forward as I race along an ever shifting maze
of shrinking convolutions to find a hidden prize.

Each day *The* pauses grow louder,
become the rattle of jailer's keys
warning me of the silent isolation cell
that follows *The.*

precedes some lost before my ends.

hangs

in between us as I search my messy of
to find a more specific than

a single, but definite, demanding
I step forward as I race along an ever shifting
of shrinking to find a hidden

Each grow louder,
become the of
warning me of the silent
that follows

~ ED WILSON

One Day Before
Threescore and Ten

One day left in my sixties,
one day left to count down
(trembling on the stand)
to launch what may remain.

One day left to contemplate
where the years have gone
seven decades like missions—
successful or star-crossed.

One day, and four hours of that
now spent on sleep, or musing
on some interstellar song
searching for its lost refrain.

One day to find the payload
floating on the ocean
one day to rescue someone
unmindful of the cost.

One day left to redeem errors
fire the rockets now to burn
the flotsam and the jetsam
engines roaring with sustain.

One day, any day, May Day
Twirling beyond Mars
Beeping a persistent signal:
All is not lost; all is not lost.

~ JIM FERGUSON

MORNINGS WITH MAX

Each morning in my study
we share a common hour,
he stretched across the armchair,
head resting on his paws,
me seated at the desk,
head anchored in the clouds.

In him exist ancestral wolves,
who made accommodations
to predators who
wielded stones, crafted spears,
and shared their kills.

Each of us is serious
in our special ways.
He can smell a rainbow,
while I contemplate our days,
yet here we share a common peace.

The time has passed.
He licks my hand —
his gentle way to take command.
He tells me that not just he, but We,
must go outside to bark at squirrels
or maybe just to take a pee.

~ ED WILSON

Seasoned

July, yet I feel summer slipping away
as daylight hours pass their zenith
and the doldrums of August lie ahead.
The solstice cast a foreshortened shadow,
a naked mast inscribed upon a silver sea.
Today I saw a golden leaf fall
landing on the bower of a branch below.
Only one, yes, but soon enough
the sun begins its autumnal slide.
Then days, like years, will faster pass
advancing like an arctic front—
to crystallize December morns,
to settle winter in my bones.

~ Jim Ferguson

I Fear the Loss of Words with Time

so I must tell you that I love you now
   before all my words have flown.
Each day it seems another leaves.
Child, find my words.
Play with each sweet one.
Release them to fly away and
   return to land softly on the ear.
Each child must find the words for love.

Each child must find the words for love.
Release them to fly away and
   return to land softly on the ear.
Play with each sweet one.
Child, find my words.

Perhaps I left a word upon the lawn
   before I fell asleep.
Each day it seems another leaves,
so I must tell you that I love you now
   before all my words have flown.

~ ED WILSON

Extra Innings for Joe Morgan

When he was a Colt 45-er,
he would have just
flopped to the ground, limp,
and maybe laughed,
if someone like Gibson
had come in high
and tight with that fearful
familiar heater.
Sweeping legs from underneath his
crouched body, dodging a
Conigliaro fate –
eye swollen shut,
mind forever bruised.
He'd try it now,
not because he wanted to.
but it was the only play
left in him – the dusty champ,
the faded Big Red MVP.

Perhaps, he'd let Tom Terrific
hurl baseball justice in his defense,
send a message to the likes of
Garcia or Kaline
that there are rules,
and then there are the rules.
The old-timers should
damn well know better --
let the man take
his dignified final trot
around the bases.

But the last pitch curves unhittable,
for all; and Seaver's arm, it was toast,
as was his hip and his mind.
He'd been waiting in the pen
for his turn for so long now
he'd forgotten how to
grip the two-seamer or the
four-seamer… or how to even
swallow his pride.

Man, he'd been terrific in his
Metropolitan days.
Precise.
Graceful.
Strong.
Then, he could outrun Rose.
Now, he couldn't even outpace
a crowned virus.

But the game plays on
with bases loaded,
down by two.
And Joe couldn't speak of
how his body ached,
how arms and heart
ignored his requests.
His best, final swing –
the quiet final breeze,
taking one last pitch,
one for the team.
And let the litter carry him
down the lines,
waved finally, peacefully home.

Someone else would have to
step up to bat.
Larkin waiting on deck,
Junior in the hole --
they'd be equal to
the Gibsons, Gossages or Saberhagens
and send the game
into extra innings.

~ MEL CAMPBELL

SNOW DAY

Como Mississippi is a long way
from Aspen Colorado.
There aren't any ski slopes,
hardly a hill.

Snow has no value,
unless you are a child,
too young to worry
about feeding cows
and frozen pipes.

A few inches of snow in Mississippi
        and, baby, you got yourself a snow day!

We didn't have slopes,
we had Uncle Bob.
With a makeshift sled
hooked to his truck's trailer hitch,
he dragged us around town,
slid us around corners.

When Papa found out, he wanted to cut
Uncle Bob's limb off the family tree.
But every kid needs an Uncle Bob
to turn a little snow into a lifetime memory.

~ ED WILSON

BOUQUET

Rachel asks me to take her to lunch
Every time I call, but then is too nervous to go
When I arrive.

        Alzheimer's progresses that way,

        I suppose, I reply, watching my wife

        Rearrange a week-old rosy bouquet.

I'm so sorry to hear about Daniel's death,
She tells me. Such an old, old friend.

        Third one of my '59 class

this summer.
She begins removing a few wilted flowers
from the vase.

        Couldn't you put an aspirin

        in the clean water?

It helps when they're fresh;
Now? I don't know.

        Cut the stems back a bit,

        I plead, so the remaining ones

        Might last.

We gaze at the nine left from the dozen
Roses so bright only a few days ago.
Hints of black discolor edges of petals.
Are they worth keeping?
She asks.

        I cannot answer.

~ STEVE COLEMAN

Love

THE MOUNTAIN

The mountain is ours.
It endures like stone
for as long as stone endures.

The mountain moves between us.
Outward the shores erode.
We hang on but apart.

Whether we hold on—
or drop into the sea—
the mountain remains

Sufficient in its solitude.
The mountain moves between us.
The mountain is not ours.

~ JIM FERGUSON

HOW YOU WALK

You now lead.
It has not always been so.
It was he who set the pace.
Raked the leaves.
Changed the tires.
Chopped the firewood.
Carried you over the threshold.
Hoisted the heavy Christmas boxes.
Pushed the new fridge in a hand truck.
Put the four-year-old
on his shoulder and carried him
upstairs to bed.

On the path,
you twist and turn wince-free.
Thick-soled sneakers,
over-sized shades
and sculpted leggings
your stylish accessories.
His short-sleeved shirt
hangs over his trousers.
Leather shoes hold his sockless feet.
His movement that
of someone getting
reacquainted with walking
now that his skin
has turned to wood.

As you round a corner,
you pause and turn
toward the afternoon sun.
He is not there yet.
But when he arrives,
you will be ready
to lift him up
with the brightest of smiles.

~ TOM GORDON

THE CIRCLE

In the square corners of the world,
where whispers dance like shadows,
there exists a tale woven of halves and circles,
giving and receiving.

Two souls in the corner of a room,
their hearts entwined
in a delicate dance
of trust and hesitation.

"I give you half of me," whispered one,
her voice carrying the weight of dissolution.
"No more, lest I should lose
my certainty."

"For your sake, for my sake, half will I take.
But only if you receive half of me
so we each continue to grow full circle."
He said in reply.

"Half I'll take and give, for he who gives gives all
By halves, cannot live; then let the barrier fall.
As two separate circles we each shall love,
our shared parts will help us grow."

And so, the barriers erected by fear and doubt
crumble like ancient ruins under the weight
of truth and love. In the embrace of a shared
eternal circle, they found growth and completeness.

For in the giving of oneself partially
they discovered the boundless beauty
of unity and the infinite depths of their
shared existence.

Their love becomes a symphony,
each note resonating with the harmony
of two souls merged as one,
yet as separate as two circles.

In that sacred space, where halves dissolved
into shared wholes,
and back into separate circles,
they find their home, their sanctuary,
their everlasting separateness.

~ ROGER CARLISLE

MOTHER'S DAY GRATITUDE

If I am worth anything,
I can trace some of it to that day in the grocery store
when, after my usual mixed success in adding
extra Oreos or ice cream
to your cart, I stood in the checkout line
and watched you tell the cashier,
'You're very pretty.'
In reply, the lady not only said 'Thank you.'
She said it with surprise in her voice
and a brightening in her face.

I think there was power
in your generous gesture.
I would like to think that cashier
later took a look in her rear view mirror
and smiled that someone had noticed
what she dared not say publicly about herself.

And perhaps, when she got home,
your kindness was part of the day's memory
she shared with her husband, prompting him
to put his arms around her in agreement
while inwardly vowing to atone for the times
he had neglected to tell her himself.

And maybe the memory of your three words
had the kind of shelf life
that led her to say complimentary things
to strangers or reaffirm love
to those who needed it.

For all the times we mouth the golden rule,
we fail nearly as often to carry it out.
Still, your lesson to me
from that long-ago Saturday
is that every checkout line,
every human encounter,
is a chance at redemption.

~ TOM GORDON

PLATONIC LOVE

Marsilio Ficino, the name says it all—
Doctor, poet, priest, philosopher
Astrologer and first interpreter
Of *all* of Plato's works into Latin.
Yet he still found the time
To coin the term *Platonic Love*
And place it as the top rung
On what he called the ladder of love.

Thanks a lot, Marsilio.

~ JIM FERGUSON

BUSTER AND LOOSEY

"Your cat," my neighbor says,
"Loosey still comes to see me."
"I know she likes to visit your cat,"
I reply. "They seem such good friends."

"But Buster died, you see,
Some seven months back,
Or something like that.
Very persistent, your black and white cat."

"Oh, I hope she's not a bother,"
I apologize. "Just shoo her away."
"We don't let her out
In baby-bird season anyway."

"She climbs on the ledge
Of our kitchen window,"
He explains, "peers in
And scratches on the glass pane."

"Perhaps she doesn't know
Our Buster has died.
No bother to us that she comes,
I just hate to see her disquieted."

"Perhaps I should keep her in
For a few days," I suggest.
"Maybe she'll then forget Buster,
And put her cat-mind at rest."

Now Loosey stands and meows
On the inside of our door,
Wanting out to return
To our neighbor's once more.

"You mustn't bother our neighbors,
Loosey," I tell her,
"Buster's not there.
You'll have to stay here."

She then looks at me,
Yellow eye slits grow wider;
"Did he die--my Buster?
What's the meaning of that?"

I stare back at Loosey
What do you say to a kitty?
Of life, of death,
Of love, of loss, or pity?

~ Steve Coleman

LEGACY

To Mama Bear

You taught me to listen to water.
To leave undisturbed
the whispers of streams.
To discern a symphonic fanfare
in a run of rapids.
To hear unseen hands
applauding our presence
at a stony river bend.
To kneel reverently, touch the surface,
and revel in the ripple of deep pools.
To let my soul lie
in a midrib of a maple leaf
and float in eager acceptance
to an unknown terminus.

Whenever, wherever I hear
the flow of water,
I will seek its source,
think of you,
search the canopy above
for the eyes of an owl,
and wait for its silent wings
to carry me home.

~ TOM GORDON

Castello di Postignano

For Leah

Every summer your great grandma
made us climb halfway into
the Carolina blue sky
to look for blueberries on *Satulah*,
a Cherokee word I think means
Mountain Where Everything Grows,
Except Blueberries.

She found berries there once.
So she kept trying, defying logic
and the definition of insanity.

Which might explain why
I'm at another writing retreat,
this time at a castle, a real one,
learning again to show, not tell.

It's the last night,
my bags are by the door.
I'm climbing the tower
to look for constellations.
I'm trying to reach you one more time.

I want to tell you how
the workmen here found frescoes
behind a collapsed wall,
a sort of architectural pentimento.
I want to show you how
the colors never faded.

I want you to know I will look
for you in the stars as I look for
you at the stars.
I will write you
though I cannot write you
back into this world.

In the beginning, shards of light
spilled across the night sky,
some too beautiful to become stars.
I will look for them behind the darkness.

~ BARRY MARKS

Struggles

A doctor after years of scientific training
finally understands depression

This is how the world feels
when the person feels insufficient.

My executive function is not filing
my life properly.

A fog, a darkness, a black dog, sink holes in solid ground,
buzzards circling, dead leaves blowing in a storm.

I dance around my depression with metaphors,
paint pictures of the pain with my words.

Time slows and every breath becomes difficult,
my chest is in a vise, I can't get out of bed.

I circle empty days on my calendar with no hope,
no plans, no purpose.

A spoon of food seems to take 20 minutes
to eat.

I fight the overwhelming emptiness by
stripping away the false and nonessential.

My best hope is every bit as likely
to occur as my worst fear.

It is time to open up and swallow my suffering,
understand the depth of my patient's pain

~ ROGER CARLISLE

The Woman at the End of the Bar Has Something to Say

Right now she is saying it
to the melted ice at the bottom of her glass.
She was drinking something brown.
You might ask her if something is wrong,
if you can help. You might try
telling her you understand.
You don't understand.
She looks like someone you know.
You don't know her.
She is wearing a nice dress.
Her hair is a little messed up,
but her nails are perfect.
Stiletto heels.
Coming from somewhere?
Going somewhere?
She's going to get up,
pay her tab,
put on her coat
and walk out into the night.
She's going to go home and kill herself.
It's better for both of you that way.
That's all she wanted to say.

~ Barry Marks

FAMILIAR ACCELERATION

The grey cinder-block bucket of blood,
A has-been honkytonk, still stands on Sand Mountain's
sleek side.
Driving up to it was curvy and treacherous, like those who
frequented the place.
The milieu of miscreants.
But it's not like the creants had somewhere better to go.

Knives and knuckles were the bloody economy
Of a dive lubricated by illegal beer, dancing and
electrified loins.
And in its day, the occasional teen would drive drunkenly
off the hill
Marking the mountain with limbs and harsh lessons;
Unwelcome drips from the bucket – venous and heinous –
That moved morality to rescuing redemption.
"No more fights. No more crashes, and senseless deaths,"
And they pointed the ignorant, poor youths to Jesus,
not Schlitz
While John Law cracked down on bootleggers, indecency
and white trash.

Later when I was a kid, a silver Mac truck careened out
of control
Down a slippery mountain four-lane
Intended to replace the old bloody byway.
Its driver was going too fast, and the rig smashed into a
loping Chevy Chevette
Lounging at a red light too close to the foot of
Sand Mountain.
Neither could get out of the way. Pieces of car, truck and
flesh flew into the air.

There was nothing to do except
Scrape the unsuspecting driver and car off Highway 431.
And point fingers at a tired, underpaid portly man
Who popped speed to feed his family.
The reds didn't press an accelerator, but blame
accelerated anyway.

They took his livelihood and more...
And built a runaway ramp – a pit of pebbles and safety
To catch big rigs barreling down the mountain decline.
And threw that stop light into a deep part of
Guntersville Lake,
While encouraging John Law to cite out-of-town hasty,
unfamiliar rulebreakers.

The ramp remains – with grass growing among the pebbles –
and the red light's back.
Cold Schlitz is legal now and on tap somewhere in town, a
welcome reminder
For the old fellows meeting at the new Jacks for breakfast.
They recall the truck, but probably not the bucket, and in
their coffee and biscuit circle,
Grasp stiffened fingers and pray for protection against
Socialists and migrant cartels and demons who would take
their rights,
As the man-made lake just beyond them awaits the
next object to
Accelerate down the side of the hill to be cast into its depths.

~ Mel Campbell

THE PRESENT

The moments of the past no longer exist.
Those of the future, yet to be.
Only this moment is real,
the sharp blade of the present
severing the non-existence of the past
from the non-existence of the future.
The magician withdraws the cleaver,
opens the box, and reveals
a buxom and bejeweled assistant,
unsevered and full of life,
transcendent in her beauty,
the present we can neither refuse,
nor grasp, the gift of reality,
relief from illusion—
the eternal Now.

~ JIM FERGUSON

LEAF AND YOU

To Beth

A leaf falls
from the highest branch
on a hardwood tree.
It touches other branches as it falls,
as if to say farewell.
The wind catches it
in a comforting caress
before it joins its confreres
on earth.

I do not clock the leaf's descent,
but it reaches its destination
faster than you
can walk to your car.
The leaf needs no help.
You need the grip
of your boyfriend's hand
to make your way
along the sidewalk.

Seasonally obedient,
the leaf had shed its green sheen.
In the grip of a season-defying invader,
you had lost your hair, your laugh,
that vocal power
my ears relish when you are home.

I want your hair, your laugh to return,
I want to once again
feel the pulse of your presence,
to watch leaves languishing in the air
as you turn the ignition key in your car,
the light from your face
a bright banner
in the chiaroscuro
of darker, shorter days.

~ TOM GORDON

PARACHUTE

"The Hun I am fighting may be calling on Him too...
How can I call on God to help me shoot
down a man in flames?"
No Parachute: A Classic Account of
War in the Air in WWI
— ARTHUR GOULD LEE, AIR VICE-MARSHAL,
ROYAL AIR FORCE

You know this place.
Gray-stubbled men surround an oil drum fire,
most in tattered charnel house coats,
blowing into their hands and doing
that dance men do when the cold
sinks its spurs in their bones.
That one there, closest the fire, the one not
dancing but glowering in his chair, empty
pants legs clipped shut, green jacket
whispering a faded name.
That one calls to you.
You know what he is going to say, don't you?
How if his first prayer were answered,
the bastards would know because his legs would grow back
and he would kick their sorry asses from Kabul to
Kingdom Come,
then get to work on their children.
And what can you say?
It is not the bare concrete chill of November

that makes you shudder as you walk from the fire.
It is what you know. What you always knew.
You walk past St. Stephen's and Beth Israel, First
Calvary and the library and the market and the graveyard.
You raise up your grief and your voice but you hear
only shivering stars in a barren sky:

> *What is sadder than dying old?*
> *More deadly than the devil you see?*
> *What God do you fear*
> *more than the One who will not*
> *answer the prayers of the righteous?*

~ BARRY MARKS

PIPPA'S DITTY

What brewed in Browning's brain
when he penned *Pippa's Song*,
asserting God to be "in his heaven"
and all to be "right with the world"?

In verse an idyllic garden is laid,
as British troops butchered throngs
of *Paddies*, *Pakis* and *Kaffirs**, even
as indentured bagpipes skirled.

If such a god is in heaven perhaps
she is not at present in the world, and
we poor monkeys might catch a break.

~ J. SHANNON WEBSTER

* pejorative British slang for ethnic folk

CARDINAL

Outside, the cardinal stops, bewildered.
Its feathers recede

into themselves until it no longer
burns with color. It shrinks

as its beak melts and its head
folds into its chest. Its wings

tuck into its body. It turns liquid
and just as it separates into yellow

and white, a shell swallows
the cardinal and the life it owned.

I crumple the note you left into a ball
and place it gently on the bed.

~ BARRY MARKS

NOTHING

Nothing… is that a thing?
Logic dictates against it.
No thing.

"What are you doing?"
"Nothing."
Not true. You sit, listen,
you answer questions.

Is nothing the opposite of something?
Solely deletion of everything?
Can it be the opposite of anything?
Or would that make it something?

If I name it does it become a thing?
Emptiness. Absence. Vacuity.
Can nothing have properties, or Form?

What can be said about nothing. . . ?"
Physicist, "the absence of something."
Genesis, "The earth was without form, and void."
Sports Commentator, (" . . . ")

Or Quantum theory – Heisenberg's principle:
    "Nothing certain to speak of. "
Theologian: "In the beginning, God…":
Rod McKuen: (" . . . ")

What if nothing and something cancel
out everything? Is anything left?

Nothing may be sundry things to different people.
Only poets can handle this one…

> He stroked condensation on the glass,
> and as afore swore the drink his last,
> in a long, long, long line.

She did not look back or raise her voice, nor
this time slam the door, but near noiseless
quietly closed it, and left for sure.

The surgeon came to the waiting room where
parents kept long watch, and there he
merely mixed his tears with theirs, to say…

~ J. SHANNON WEBSTER

POTATOES

On crisp fall evenings,
When the moon was large
And stomachs stood at attention
For nightly inspection,
Mom would send me
To the shed out back for potatoes –
Ones we'd pulled from
Clay soil on Independence Day
(Because we always dug potatoes then).

She seemed to enjoy sending me
To the dingy, tin-topped out building,
Where my father and grandfather also worked
Wood and lumber into cabinets
And furniture.

She lessened her burden by sending a boy
Because no man would likely do it.
It was just the time and the tide.
She loathed the dank, earthy smelling building,
Especially at night – the home to spiders,
snakes and devilments
Of unnamable number.

Often, I delivered my quarry
Only to be sent back...
For better ones, bigger ones,
ones that were not rotting or sprouting.

Taters are sneaky bastards.
Lying in the quiet,
Sprouting eyes, leaves and
Shooting here and there.
Holding themselves to
The ground for dearest of life.

I'd dream that they were waiting,
Quietly in the shed,
To attack gangly boys out
To take one – or four – of their own.
And build up some childish
Resentment at being interrupted in
My attention to the castaways on
Gilligan's Island.

"Why me?"
"Because it's your job. Because you can.
You're a part of the family."

Eventually, she'd be satisfied
And turn the tubers into
Meat and potato casserole.
And over the years, bellies
Would get fatter and older.

We haven't picked potatoes
In 40 years from the field
That now is grass and adolescent
Skinny pecan trees.

And the shop now only holds
Rusting and dusty
Bikes and hoes and ghosts
Of those no longer
Working in the smells of
Sawdust and grease.

Today, she hands
the plastic urinal that my
Dad uses, since he hasn't left
The bed in months,
His room smelling earthy
And dank, of urine and decay.
She points me to the toilet
To empty the container,
As she likely
Has done 100 times now,
And may do 100 more
Before she dutifully tells
Him, "Goodnight, my darling,"
And kisses his bedhead white hair.
For what might then
Be the final time.

~ MEL CAMPBELL

NO ONE LOVES YOU

The dog who follows you home would
follow anyone eating a candy bar.
The priest who listens,
then grades your confession.
The God who loves everyone,
so what ?
No one loves you.

The son only a mother could love.
The mother.
Your *friends* list on Facebook
(Happy Birthday!)
All the offers addressed to you
or *Current Resident.*

The women, satisfied.
Your entire Christmas list.
Everyone loves you, congratulations!
No one loves you
so, what?

DNA, Inc. can draw your face
and tell you which monkey is your very own.
A drone can find you.
Turn on Location Accuracy.
Allow to Track.
Everyone knows about you.
No one knows you, so
no one loves you
So what?

~ Barry Marks

LAST VISIT

Resting in chair, gazed out
window to right. Red flowers
shined in bright sun, blue
sky smiled behind green trees.

Call disrupted. Son of
friend advising mom at
hospital,
      not well,
           may be the end.

Ask, can we visit?
Yes.
Dress.

Took journey cannot avoid.
Arrived,
Found room.
Door closed.
Paused,
Took breath,
Knocked.
Door opened.

Three children.
Friend in bed.
Eyes closed.
Mouth open.
Hands shaking.

Hugs around,
whispered conversations,
we turned heads from
she we came to see.
Silence filled the room.

Youngest son sat to
hold shaking hand.
Daughter, middle child,
turned away, tears in eyes.
Oldest child, a son,
Seemed calm.

Will visit bring peace?
Returned home to rest. Gazed
out window to right, sun bright,
red flowers. sky blue.

~ NICK GAEDE

(A Dream) Of Mud and Mouthpieces

When I opened the case,
    the worn black and green
    felt squished, soaked
    by water and mud
        I would be late for the performance
        And I hadn't played or practiced
        my King Silver Flair trumpet since 2018.
I'd been running, not winded
    turned a corner
    found the band milling
    casually playing warm-ups
    solo, not ensemble

B-flat concert scales, arpeggios,
    and brassy show-offs
    wasting their high notes
    to impress flutists
    who couldn't care less

The silver, 12B mouthpiece was still
    in its pocketslot, wet
    spattered with mire,
    like my trusty harmon mute.
    And the unused 7C
    Deeper inside, muck encased.
    (Didn't need it anyway; only newbies use that size)

And the band was lining up, waiting for me
        to begin the performance,
        though I wasn't sure
        what we were playing
        or where I'd find a uniform
        that fit
                I guess I'd wing it,
                like always.

~ MEL CAMPBELL

WARBLER

Once, in Auschwitz,
amid human screams,
barking commands, growling dogs,
flesh-tinged smoke, necks in nooses,
and firing squads,
a warbler built a home.

It answered no command
but a deeply wrinkled dictate
compelling it to take wing,
build nests,
raise young,
protect them from predators,
find them food for firm footing
in the waiting, uncertain world.

How could it have known
what its song and dance
would mean to a girl
struggling to stand erect
in a footprint-covered courtyard,
trying to hold firm
against the heavy hand of fate?

~ TOM GORDON

WHAT'S IT ALL ABOUT?

Listen up, Alfie.
You still think real men need
Guts 'n Glory?

You can chuck out Glory with your
baseball cards, jockstrap, and daddy's
Playboys; nobody mentions
that the last dragon packed it up
while Sir Lancelot was Gloriously
banging Guinevere.

Glory is for those thumb-sucking
valedictorians goose-stepping
the lemming trail, not the guy
who knows an A- is as good as an A+ ;
because it's all pass-fail, anyway.

Without Glory, everything you thought
was Guts drops like a Pennsylvania
Legionnaire's life expectancy.

The guy with Guts isn't the fool
on the high wire, or riding shotgun
on a load of nitroglycerin,
not the guy waving his M-16
or flopping his guts on a live grenade.

Guts move the stink
that makes life work;
Glory keeps your head
above the rim.

The guy with Guts 'n Glory?
Try the 23d lemming from the left,
the one who is going to aim for
a rock ledge a third of the way down
and try, against all instinct and most logic,
to clamber back up,
square his rodent shoulders,
face east,
and stare down the sunrise.

~ BARRY MARKS

EVE'S REACH

There is a fault in northern Tanzania.
Possibly more than one, but not of this kind.
Rather a thirty-mile section of the Great Rift
that reaches up through Kenya to Ethiopia,
where a prehistoric Afarensis dubbed "Lucy"
was unearthed in 1974.

Scientists don't always spell well, not even
the famed Leakeys, which explains how
Tanzania's Oldupai became "Olduvai" Gorge.
The Gorge bore volcanic ash, gold mines,
 and cattle trails before yielding paleo finds
two million years old, extinct apes to humans.

Is it mere fancy or is it real, to feel ghosts?
The wind off the Serengeti whispers riddles
deep in the gorge, where the air lies heavy.
Why came you here to see an old ditch?
What do you not know?
Where are you going now?

Two million years ago,
the first Homo Habilis who could
looked up into a tree,
saw fruit, and she thought:

… if I could just get my hind legs under me
I would…eat…that…apple.

~ J. SHANNON WEBSTER

MIDWATCH

Midwatch alone
ninety nautical miles
east of Cape May
Others sleeping below
trusting my sixty
years at the helm

No reef in the main
the jib is flying
Frothy dark swells
send the fifty-foot sloop
gently pitching then rolling

How silent the ocean
rare slap of a wave
or dolphin's snatched breath
riding wake at the bow

Sailing a rhumb line
steering by compass
to destination vacation
My destiny less certain

Instruments' red glow
reflect off foaming
dark waves
reefs and shoals
seem to rise
from black depths
of the ocean

Freshening wind blowing
heeling the boat
Lose grip on the wheel
slip over the side
if I might--
gathered into the tide

My call unheard
in the dark
careless sea
I and my troubles
would sink
and be gone

Yet lifting my eyes
to unfathomable sky
Milky Way galaxy
sparkling orbs

So infinite mind's reflection
so strong heart's longing
I reach out so far
for a great cluster of stars
and sweep them all up
in the palm of my hand

~ STEVE COLEMAN

Humor

GOLIATH OF GATH

I know what it says in your Junior Bible Study Booklet,
but that's not how it all went down.
First of all, Goliath was not from Gath;
nobody is from Gath,
The alliteration simply improves the drama.
Secondly, it *is* drama: Think "Andre the Giant."
Lastly, David was no sweet, tow-headed shepherd boy.
Jesse's youngest was a bit of a rounder –
think Paul Newman in "Hud."

The armies were drawn up opposing each other
with a valley in-between, on a day hot as blue blazes.
The Philistines lolled in the unruly mob they were,
killing time with pissing contests and trading slugs.
Except for Goliath, that is, who they had stuffed
into bronze helmet and body armor.

The Israelite Defense Force stood motionless in the sun
in exact, orderly, ranks – Eagle Scouts to a man.
Except David, who fishtailed up late in a dust cloud,
in a white 1958 drop-top Cadillac Coupe DeVille.
He crawled over the driver's side door (window down),
with a sling shot tucked into his Tony Lama boots,
shrugging off the offered bronze helmet.

Goliath lumbered into the valley (he was big 'un) and
rested a huge sword on a broad shoulder.
David popped a strip of Wrigley's spearmint in his mouth,
leaned down to pull the slingshot from his boot
and pick up a rock.

He pulled down his sunglasses and pointed a finger
at the low-hanging limb of a cedar 50 yds away.
3 swings of the sling, he let the stone sing,
so hard, so fast, so cool that it
severed the limb right off the tree.

Goliath stood quiet for a full minute, thinking
(Hooh-leee Shee-it. They've got missiles!)
He pulled his helmet off with one hand,
and with the other tossed aside his sword,
And he spake unto Dave, "You wanna grab lunch?"
And David said, "Sure. We can take my ride."

And so it was.
Now ain't that a better ending?

~ J. SHANNON WEBSTER

LOW VOLUME

Comfortably seated in Sunday situation
I was subjected to a biblical quotation.
The minister convening this confabulation
Said, "Please bow your heads.
My words will soon come
A prayer to intone at low volume."
Hmmm, I wondered,
What might be his question?
Or is it merely an uttered oblation,
Benign in import as in solving equations?
Certainly not Baptistic brimstone fire,
Not Catholic dogma nor Elective ire?
T'was a homily mild,
Episcopally trivial—
A supplication to God
With a feeling convivial.
Awakening then suddenly
I guessed at the gist—
This somnambulistic show,
Which replayed like streaming
In tempo allegro:
Softly, sweetly but lively—
Audition from God
So pleasant to know.
Ergo invoked, I prayed
In volume so low.

~ STEVE COLEMAN

On "Being Yourself"

"Just be yourself," the counselor says.
Well *there's* a terrible idea.
Were I to *do* that, you wouldn't like it.

To the point, the world seems rudely changed.
All is now self-referential;
the sole pronoun that survived is "me".

Life is littered with self-importance.
I know; I saw it on TeeVee.
The pronoun that failed the cut was "we".

Office warning: "She's not herself today."
Thank God! Who is she *any* day?
And who gets to say who she is?

Awhile back I stopped being myself,
and declared myself a poet.
My lines have been decanting for years.
Best not stand in front of them.

~ J. Shannon Webster

My Unserious Friend

My friend ordered some German food online.
The sauerkraut has arrived but the wurst is yet to come.

My friend accidentally drank a bottle of invisible ink.
Now he's in the hospital, waiting to be seen.

My friend has been stealing the wheels off police cars.
Police are working tirelessly to catch him.

When my friend was younger, he had a job as a
Shop window mannequin. He held that position for a
long time.

My friend knew nothing when he was hired at the
local gallows.
But now he's got the hang of it.

My friend threw a party for all the contractors who helped
build his house.
The door guy showed up late. But he really knew how to
make an entrance.

My friend can walk up two flights of stairs with no problem.
But three? That's another story!

My friend tried to write a serious poem.
The verse is yet to come.

~ Jeff Book

AN ODE TO COCA COLA™

Sweet child of an Atlanta druggist,
bride of pope Asa Chandler,
mother of Dasani™, Sprite™, and Fanta™,
your blend of kola nuts and coca leaves
sustained my childhood days
with my best friend, Ernest,
washed down Ritz Crackers™
from his father's grocery store.

Hero of a thousand courtrooms,
union buster in many lands,
you carved a path to corporate glory,
dressed Santa Claus in red.
I have a bizarre desire to
share you with the world,
your empire with unsetting sun,
where melodies are sweet,
but your high fructose corn syrup
is sweeter.
A million dentists sacrifice at your altar.

In your glass bottle wisdom
you tutored me in desire,
gave me the ideal of the female form.
        (Although I've never understood
        why the hips are at the bottom.)
Those were days when time moved slowly.
We aged together, changed together—
        you in shiny cans and plastic,
        a glistening nude Adonis
        emerging from your secret pool
        in a hidden glade
        and me in saggy skin.

Your soul is effervescence,
while mine is senile plaques and amyloid deposits.
As my generation returns to dust,
you will endure to share your
Real Magic™ with a thirsty world
where Coke™ is truth, truth Coke™.

~ ED WILSON

*Note: This product is not endorsed by either
John Keats or Coca Cola™.*

PLUTO'S KEYS

In the early grey mist
As exhaust and exhaustion embrace
Wayfarers wandering streets and alleys,
Bouncing between bed sheets and
The bountiful boredom of dusty boardrooms
And boutiques,
Pluto collects his coins.

As surely as life and death,
He spins his wheel of keys
Unlocking each meter,
Where mortals buy time on earth
To protect their car semi-children.

At each stop, fat Pluto stops,
Unlocking,
Locking,
Collecting
Consigning.
Squatty short legs powering
The steely buggy onward.

No citations
Does Pluto distribute;
He calmly collects … moments
That the unsuspecting masses
Have bartered for seeming safety,
Renting rights and legality
From the tormented realm.

And he hums a spiritual,
Familiar and distant,
As quarters and dimes
Trickle like surprised souls --
A menagerie of value, evermore fleeting –
Damned to the bowels
Of a vault-locked cart,
Rolling on small rubber wheels.

Until -- a pole married to malfunction,
Where no fares are collected and the crafty
Can shake their fists at the sky
In defiance of ineluctable tolls.
Persuaded, they no longer need,
Nor recognize
These gods.

Thus, from his ring,
Pluto a newer key produces,
Etched like the ancients.
And unlocks a pouch from
His portly potbelly.
A sign, surreptitious he
Slathers over the meter-face,
For all who park there:
"Now pay with the app."

And with renewed smile,
He smooths the sticker
With the back of the brassy key,
Before also applying it
To the shiny grey paint
Of the Lexus parked therewith.

~ MEL CAMPBELL

WAITING AT THE DMV

I visited hell a few months ago
when I went to the Department of Motor Vehicles
to register my car. I was overwhelmed with a
feeling of helplessness.

I entered the DMV, the clerk said,
"Take a number and get in line!"
I was in purgatory, standing in a line
of tormented souls, waiting for our numbers to be called.

This line was longer than the line to the women's
restroom at a football game,
people were unshaven and disheveled,
gnashing their teeth, eating candy bars.

I'm the anti-hero, I avoid the cannon's mouth,
come back when everyone else is tired,
live to fight another day. I was
feeling powerless, guilty, hunkered down.

I met an elderly man who had been
standing in line for 2 weeks to register his
Volkswagen bus. After 30 days and 30 nights
of waiting, I was called to approach the teller window.

I told the clerk I wanted to register my car.
She managed to say her next sentence in one,
eye-rolling sigh. "Do you have proof of registration?"
I explained that, "NO I didn't have any registration."

It was an old car I inherited from my grandmother. She answered, and I quote: "Sir, the car must be registered before we can register it."

~ ROGER CARLISLE

Kentucky Spirits

In Newport, once a capital of vice,
A craft distillery ages its booze
In an old trolley barn painted black.
When the temperature soars, the barrels
Give up heady vapors—the angel's share.
Some whiskey lost to the barrel—the devil's cut.

On northern Kentucky's Bourbon Trail,
You're never far from the whiskey river,
The Ohio, the way frontier booze
Floated on flatboats to New Orleans.
In 1791, when Hamilton taxed spirits
Appalachia erupted; Washington
(Who made his own at Mount Vernon)
Sent troops to quash the Whiskey Rebellion.

Royce Neeley's people kept up the fight,
A hundred years of making hooch in a
Kentucky holler, battling G-men and rivals.
Jail was their tax, a stint in limbo.
Time in that barrel—the devil's share.
Now he's legit, his distillery hard by
The NASCAR track in Sparta, temple
To a sport rooted in running 'shine.

At Boone County Distilling, co-founder
Josh Quinn was a G-man, of the FBI.
Another Scots-Irish whiskey ace?
Not quite: During Passover,
Quinn the Jew must rid himself of
Hametz, the fermented grains
That rarefy in the alembic.
For the season he sells his stake
To his Gentile partner
For ten dollars—the angel's cut.

~ JEFF BOOK

THE MEANING OF LIFE

He appears bleary-eyed
At each morning's table;
"The meaning of life,
Dear Wife?
Oh, tell if you're able."

> "You ask me that question,
> Near every day.
> Eat your eggs,
> Silly husband.
> It'll all be okay."

"But what is my purpose?
Life grows ever shorter;
So much
Left undone,
It's all in disorder."

> "You've had a career,
> Made lots of money;
> We own
> Our own home,
> Stop worrying, honey."

"But I'm troubled, my dear,
You know what I mean;
What do others think?
Do I command their esteem?"

"Now, look here, darling,
If I must explain,
You're only raising
Your blood pressure.
With nothing to gain."

"I could write a novel;
Yes, maybe I should.
But character?
Plot?
Suppose it's no good?"

"Then, for God's sake, dear husband,
Go paint a nice picture.
Try your hand at sculpture,
But be Careful, darling!
A blood vessel could rupture."

"Oh, well, dear wife,
What you're conveying,
Is 'Just enjoy life,'
And old-folks kind of playing.

~ STEVE COLEMAN

Dew Drop Inn Breakfast

It's a surly-morning breakfast
at the Dew Drop Inn Motel.
I'm next to the lobby where
a chair is there, and I settle
in the metal with a piping
warm cup of coffee.

The wait staff is proving
that they can indeed wait,
so I peruse the menu's five
options, and opt for bacon
scraps and scruffled eggs.

I study the rank of breakfast
chums as we linger together
for food to come, and rate
them on a scale sullen to vacant.

True to her title the waitress waits,
short even of plates to shuffle.
In the next room the manager has

left his desk, I guess so-as not to
run the risk of making eye contact

I gave up on the scruffled eggs and
head for my car, the room key left
on the manager's bar, no receipt.
The highway tells me to leave this
behind, and let the mile markers
carry the load. I can always
buy new hubcaps somewhere
down the road.

~ J. Shannon Webster

For Feynman

"Physics is like sex: sure, it may give some practical results, but that's not why we do it."

— Richard Feynman

Outside, the midday sun
Strafes the boulevard.
In the velveteen gloom
Of this L.A. strip club,
The Professor, ringside,
Doodles on a napkin,
Inscribing the universe.

Warmed by his presence,
Eclipsed by his genius,
I observe the pole dancer's
Spatial dynamics,
Her celestial orbs.
The great man pays
Little heed but tips her:
G-string theory.
She flashes a smile, then
Pauses to plug the jukebox.
You said physics is not the
Most important thing, love is.
The Stones play Satisfaction,
Bass pulsing like a quasar.

A ceiling fan stirs the
Dark matter around us.
You said God was invented
To explain mystery. The
Truth, you said, always
Turns out to be simpler
Than we thought.
The dancer twirls, a show
Of centrifugal force.
The pole displays stasis
(An erection of more than
Four hours). If the
Droplets on my glass
Froze forever, I wonder,
Would that be hyperstasis?
The Prof proceeds
To sketch the dancer.

You said nature's imagination
Is far better than ours.
But imagine we must as
The dancer, inverted,
Mocks the laws of gravity
And demonstrates
Another thing you said:
All mass is interaction.

~ Jeff Book

WHO SHOT JOHN?

Who shot ole John
At Chez Fonfon?
A mean, sorry guy--
A likely ex-con.
Been drinking whiskey
Bottled in Bond.
John knew his killer?
No witness let on.

Steak-knife stabbed?
No, Shot by gun--
Murdered over oysters,
And Beef Wellington.
As for dessert?
Le gateau á chiffon?
Evil connoisseur!
Villanous gourmand!

So ran the blood,
From the floor-lain John.
Completely unnoticed
'Til a quarter to one.
Ladies stepped over--
Both brunettes and blonds.
Men kicked him aside
Callous as mafia dons.

An unsolved case—
Mystery goes on.
Terrible thing
So blatantly wrong?
Whoever, whoever.
Whoever shot John?
Dreadful things happened
A' la Chez Fonfon.

~ STEVE COLEMAN

In Memorium
To Two Of
Our Own

THE PAROLE OFFICER

There is nothing like a lengthy hike on a country road
To strengthen my legs and deepen my lungs
To unleash my mind to roam like a faithful dog lunging
Into the bush and back again, nose to the ground.

This morning is sunny and crisp, the sky above a vivid blue,
While around its margins drift pillows of billowy white
Cloudbanks with dark underbelly. The deciduous trees
Along the roadway, skeletal a month ago, are now clothed

With tiny leaves the understory is thick with dogwoods and redbuds
In full regalia, and pines and cedars, a profusion of green. In
the valley,
A thousand feet below, a train rumbles by—a plaintive whistle cry
at each crossing.
I swing my staff, lengthen my stride, pick up the pace,
matching the march

From boot camp remembered from long ago. I've hiked each day for
four weeks,
But for those days when rain fell, and I've built a fire each morning,
A roaring fire to sit before, sipping my coffee and reading a novel.
My wife comes in and says, "Good Morning." I smile.

This is a lifestyle we've never before known, though we've owned
A small cabin atop Lookout Mountain for many years.
A weekend visit is all we've ever had time for, and this was a first.
My birthday was early March with a week in Mentone.

No newspapers. We avoided the news all the while the Coronavirus
Was advancing. Our daughter called, said we couldn't come home,
That we must shelter in place, that Mentone is the place
We must shelter. She was insistent daily, and dramatic.

The phone rang this morning. I looked at my wife inquiringly
As she lifted the phone, and I whispered, "Who is it?"
Covering the mouthpiece with her hand, she said, "My
Parole Officer,"
And then into the receiver, "Yes, Natalie, we're still here."

So here we are in the clean air of the country. I've worn jeans
Every day for a month. We cook, she sews, I hunch over my desk
Praying for my muse to sit and stay a spell, and when she
fails to show,
I take to the road with my staff in hand, notebook in pocket,

And backpack heavy as an infantryman's load.
Though not visible, it rests on my shoulders nonetheless,
My distress is that others struggle with anxieties and depression
And nowhere to go, as I shelter in comfort.

I am an urbanite; I love cities; I love to walk on busy city
sidewalks.
The homeless are urbanites too. They loom on every block,
muttering,
Shuffling along, sleeping on benches, eating in doorways,
pleading with
Passersby. In the past four weeks, not a single homeless person
have I seen.

The Authorities say, "Shelter in Place under penalty of law," and I
have done so,
In a mountain retreat where the air is clear, I'm
comfortable. And yet
My pack is heavy and distracting. When every shop exhibits a sign
"For Patrons only,"
Where may the homeless wash their hands; and where indeed may
they Shelter?

~ CHERVIS ISOM

Chervis Isom grew up in Birmingham and attended
Birmingham public schools. He earned a B.A. degree from
Birmingham-Southern College (1962) and a J.D. from
Cumberland School of Law (1967). He practiced law with
Berkowitz, Lefkovits, Isom & Kushner, which in 2003 merged
with Baker, Donelson, Bearman, Caldwell, and Berkowitz.
He continued with the merged firm until his retirement in
2021. Chervis published a memoir in 2014, *The Newspaper
Boy: Coming of Age in Birmingham, Alabama During the Civil
Rights Era,* which has become a greatly significant contribution
to the history of his times. Chervis said that there is nothing he
likes better than pushing words around. He had an untimely
death on May 18, 2023 while vacationing with his family in
Chinon, France.

WITH CASEY AT THE BAT

For a third grader, the upcoming summer posed new opportunities. The one my father was pushing me toward was joining a Little League baseball team. During that school year, my mother found the poem, "Casey at the Bat" by Emest Thayer in a magazine, I think it was *The Saturday Review.* She showed it to me to encourage that baseball endeavor.

I read the poem and loved it! I tore the page out of the magazine and folded it up so 1could carry it in my hip pocket to school. I pulled the poem out to read it from time *to* time and decided that I would commit the poem to memory. I would spend time at recess out on the playground going over the poem, verse by verse, memorizing the lines. Finally, I could recite the entire poem without looking at the page.

Little League, however, was a disastrous failure. My unathletic and uncoordinated body made me even afraid to try out for a team. For the first time, 1 felt like a failure to my father and an outcast from my peers. That failed summer cast a blight upon ability to even enjoy attending a game for years to come.

It took me too long to recover from not being a baseball player, but as an adult I could look back in genuine amazement at that eight-year-old boy who imagined that he could recite such a long poem from memory. If it had been a school assignment, he might have balked, but something about that poem engaged him.

Something in him decided to rise up and do the work

needed to accomplish the task. I did not know it at the time, but that summer marked a crossroads in my life. It was like an ax, splitting away what was not in my nature and what was true to my nature. It was impossible for me to recognize at the time, or in the intervening years that followed, but it was the play of poetry that became the redeeming moment of that troublesome childhood event.

It was poetry that would continue to call at odd moments of my passage through junior high and high school. It was poetry that would say to me, "Pick up your pen and write. You can do this!"

Even if I had managed all those years ago to make the team, or even to be a star player, I doubt that at age 65 I would be looking at getting back on the baseball diamond to toss a few for the love of the game. But I can still catch a word and send it flying in a sonnet. I can field a phrase and toss it into a haiku; or send a cutter of simile along a free verse stanza.

Most redeeming of all, I can look back in admiration at that eight-year-old boy who memorized "Casey at the Bat," and say, "Great job, son! Who else could do that like you at your age?"

~ CHARLIE KINNAIRD

Charles Kinnaird was a writer whose career choices included teaching, social work, and healthcare. A native of Alabama, he also lived and worked in Hong Kong and California. He maintained a love for writing, sharing some of his poetry and essays on his blog: *Not Dark Yet* at www.notdarkyet-commentary.blogspot.com. His work has been published in the *Birmingham Arts Journal* and *Avant Appalachia*. Charlie resided in Birmingham, Alabama with his wife, Vicki, enjoying gardening and birdwatching until his unexpected early death on February 18, 2023.

Contributor
Biographies

Jeff Book, over a long career as a writer and editor, has covered travel, food, design, and other topics on six continents. His work has appeared in *Departures*, *GQ*, *Smithsonian*, *Travel & Leisure*, *Coastal Living*, *The Los Angeles Times*, *Elle Décor*, and other publications. He values poetry as a liberating use of language and a fresh window on the world.

Mel Campbell is an award-winning communicator and communications strategist by trade, with more than 30 years of experience in corporate storytelling, media relations, promotions, video production/scripting and speechwriting. In addition, he is a published author, lecturer, poet and the creator of the occasionally-updated burger review blog – Beautimous Burger (beautimousburger.wordpress.com) – which allows him to express his burger whims and whatever else strikes his fancy.

Roger Carlisle is a 77-year-old semi-retired physician, married with two children. He currently lives in Birmingham and works in a free medical clinic for the poor. He grew up in Oklahoma and was a history major in college. He has been writing poetry for 12 years and has published 57 poems in various magazines and poetry journals.

Steve Coleman, graduate of Indian Springs School and with A.B. from Duke University and an M.A. from University of Alabama, has been a naval officer, a high school teacher, a businessman, and commercial real estate broker. He has published four novels: The Navigator series, André's *Reboot: Striving to Save Humanity*, which has won Honorable Mention from Writer's Digest, a Distinguished Favorite 2021 of NYC Big Book Awards, and a Silver Medal by Independent Publisher Book Awards 2020. His screenplay of Andre's Reboot won an Honorable Mention from Santa Barbara International Screenplay Awards 2022. See www.andretherobot.com and www.captstevestories.com.

Jim Ferguson began writing poetry in grade school and has continued writing over the years while working as a student, a teacher, and a lawyer. Currently a resident of Over-the-Mountain Birmingham, he has been published in the *Birmingham Arts Journal,* the *Almost Dead Poets Society,* and has contributed to previous anthologies of the Highland Avenue Poets.

A. H. Gaede, Jr. (Nick) was born and raised in Charlotte, NC. He attended Phillips Academy Andover (1957), Yale University (BS 1961), Duke School of Law (1961, Law Review). He and his wife, Jo Anne, moved to Birmingham in 1964 where Nick worked at Bradley Arant for over 40 years. He was then briefly with BE&K, Inc. and KBR, Inc. and is now with Bainbridge Mims Rogers & Smith. He has always enjoyed reading (favorites are T. S. Eliot and Mary Oliver) and writing poems. As Eliot wrote in "Little Gidding," Nick hopes, "Every phrase and every sentence is an end and a beginning." Nick's only other published work is in legal journals and treatises.

Tom Gordon, a native of Houston, Texas, has spent most of his adult life in Alabama, working as an editor and reporter at *The Anniston Star*, and as a reporter and part-time editor at *The Birmingham News*. He has contributed articles and photos to **B Metro Magazine**, and photos and poems to the Highland Poets' previous anthologies, *The Social Distance* and *Poems for Hungry Minds*. He has poems published in *Birmingham Arts Journal* and *Aura Literary Arts Review*, and partnered with Birmingham artist Veronique Vanblaere ("Vero") on "An Artist and a Poet Walk into a Coffee Shop," a 2021 exhibition of haikus and paintings. Gordon has a bachelor's degree in political science from the University of Alabama, where he was the lead plaintiff in a 1970 lawsuit challenging the university's decision to ban Yippie leader Abbie Hoffman from speaking on campus. Tom also has a master's degree in journalism from the University of Missouri and spent the year 1981 reporting and writing in Europe and West Africa. He enjoys dancing, traveling – this year to France, last year to Vietnam and Cambodia – and singing with local jazz musicians. He also has spent countless hours watching and photographing birds.

Barry Marks is the author of four books of poetry and several chapbooks. A frequent reader and seminar leader at poetry gatherings, he is a past president of the Alabama State Poetry Society and the winner of numerous contests and awards, including Alabama Book of the Year, and a finalist for both the Eric Hoffer Grand Prize and Poetry Prize. His poetry has appeared in many journals and anthologies. His books can be found at the websites for Brick Road Poetry Press and Negativity Capability Press, as well as on Amazon. When not writing, he finds time to practice law.

J. Shannon Webster bears labels of musician and songwriter (*Heart at and Hat in Hand*, rec. Canada), *Stone* and *Silverback*s rec. at Muscle Shoals), pastor, community organizer and workshop leader. A graduate of the University of New Mexico (journalism), he earned his advanced degree at Chicago's McCormick Theological. Other writing aside, his current calling – poetry – has been published in the *New Mexico Poetry Anthology 2023*, in *Poems for Hungry Minds* by the Highland Avenue Poets, and book-length *Simulacra* by Mezcalita Press (OKC).

Ed Wilson was raised outside of Jefferson, Mississippi and currently is a resident of Birmingham, Alabama. He is a husband, a father, and is retired from practicing pathology. He devotes his time to watercolor and oil painting, failing to learn Spanish as a second language, and creative idleness.

Véronique Vanblaere, *Illustrator* – aka Véro, the traveling artist – illustrates, paints, works with fibers and fabrics, redesigns clothing, and even dabs in puppetry. For almost 30 years, this Belgian expat has lived in Birmingham, where she has developed a love-hate relationship with possums. They often appear in her sketchbooks.